easy

Chicken

easy

Chicken

MARKS &
SPENCER

Marks and Spencer p.l.c.
PO Box 3339
Chester CH99 9QS

shop online
www.marksandspencer.com

Copyright © Exclusive Editions 2007

Additional Photography by Günter Beer
Additional Food Styling by Oliver Trific
Introduction by Anne Sheasby

ISBN: 978-1-84461-981-8

Printed in China

The views expressed in this book are those of the author but they are general views only and readers are urged to consult a relevant and qualified specialist for individual advice in particular situations. Marks and Spencer p.l.c. and Exclusive Editions hereby exclude all liability to the extent permitted by law for any errors or omissions in this book and for any loss, damage or expense (whether direct or indirect) suffered by a third party relying on any information contained in this book.

NOTES FOR THE READER
This book uses both metric and imperial measurements. Follow the same units of measurement throughout; do not mix metric and imperial. All spoon measurements are level, unless otherwise stated: teaspoons are assumed to be 5 ml and tablespoons are assumed to be 15 ml. Unless otherwise stated, milk is assumed to be semi-skimmed, eggs and individual vegetables such as potatoes are medium, and pepper is freshly ground black pepper. Recipes using raw or very lightly cooked eggs should be avoided by infants, the elderly, pregnant women, convalescents and anyone suffering from an illness.

Mixed Sources
Product group from well-managed forests and other controlled sources
www.fsc.org Cert no.SGS-COC-003450
© 1996 Forest Stewardship Council
FSC

Contents

Introduction

Chicken is one of the most popular meats as it is versatile, easy to prepare, quick to cook and full of flavour. This makes it ideal as the basis for numerous tasty recipes to suit all occasions.

Chicken is an excellent source of protein and provides some vitamins, such as Niacin (a B vitamin), and minerals, such as zinc and iron (in the dark meat). It is also low in fat, especially when the skin is removed.

Buying Chicken

Most supermarkets and butchers offer a good range of chicken. When buying fresh chicken, it is advisable to look for free-range birds because their flavour is often superior to that of factory reared chicken. They will also have enjoyed a good standard of welfare, with some access to open air. Organic birds are preferred by some consumers, although they are usually the most expensive choice.

Check the 'use-by' date and choose a bird with plump breasts (rather than one that looks bony), with a firm, unblemished creamy white or yellow skin (depending on the variety). Larger birds tend to be meatier with a more developed flavour.

Buying a whole bird and cutting it into portions yourself is usually the cheapest option. However, for convenience, you may prefer to buy chicken portions (either skin on or off, on the bone or boneless), such as chicken breasts, drumsticks, thighs and wings.

Storage & Food Safety

Store fresh chicken in a loosely covered container in the refrigerator for up to 2 days. Make sure that any raw chicken is placed on a low shelf (to prevent it from dripping or leaking onto any foods below) in the coldest part of your fridge, which should be between 0°C and 5°C (32°F and 41°F). Remember that raw and cooked chicken should always be stored separately.

Fresh raw chicken can be frozen for up to 3 months and cooked chicken can be frozen for up to 2 months (in a 4-star rating freezer).

Ideally, frozen chicken should be defrosted in the refrigerator, not at room temperature, to minimise possible bacterial contamination. Defrost frozen chicken overnight in the refrigerator and always make sure it is thoroughly defrosted before you cook it (otherwise the centre may not be cooked when the outside looks done, which may lead to food poisoning). Remember, never refreeze thawed chicken.

Always wash your hands thoroughly before and after handling raw or cooked chicken, and make sure that work surfaces and utensils are cleaned with hot soapy water. Always use separate chopping boards and utensils when preparing raw and cooked chicken.

Roasting Chicken

Prepare, then weigh the whole bird (with the stuffing in place if the bird is going to be roasted stuffed), and calculate the cooking time, allowing 20 minutes per 450 g/1 lb, plus 20 minutes. Roast in a preheated oven at 220°C/425°F/Gas Mark 7, for the first 15 minutes, then reduce the oven temperature to 190°C/375°F/Gas Mark 5 for the remaining calculated time. Roast for the calculated time or until the juices run clear when the thickest part of the thigh is pierced with a fork or skewer. If the juices are pink or there are traces of blood, continue roasting the chicken until the juices run clear. Remove the chicken from the roasting tin and place on a warmed serving plate. Cover with foil and allow to rest for 10 minutes before carving.

The internal temperature of cooked chicken, should reach 80–85°C (176–185°F).

Chicken portions can be roasted at 190°C/375°F/Gas Mark 5 for about 30–45 minutes, depending on their size. Always make sure the chicken is thoroughly cooked before serving.

Adding Flavour to Roast Chicken

When roasting a whole chicken, there are several simple ways you can add flavour to the meat. For example, place a whole lemon (pierced a couple of times), a peeled onion or a few fresh herbs and peeled garlic cloves inside the cavity of the bird before roasting. Alternatively, carefully push citrus fruit slices (such as lemon, orange or lime slices) or fresh herb sprigs (such as thyme or rosemary) under the skin covering the breast, before roasting.

Flavoured butters can also be spread under the skin. Alternatively, try brushing the outside of a whole chicken with oil, then sprinkling with ground spices or dried herbs to add flavour, colour and crispness.

Soups &
Starters

Cream of Chicken Soup

serves 4

3 tbsp butter

4 shallots, chopped

1 leek, sliced

450 g/1 lb skinless, boneless chicken breasts, chopped

600 ml/1 pint chicken stock

1 tbsp chopped fresh parsley

1 tbsp chopped fresh thyme, plus extra sprigs to garnish

175 ml/6 fl oz double cream

salt and pepper

Melt the butter in a large saucepan over a medium heat. Add the shallots and cook, stirring, for 3 minutes, until slightly softened. Add the leek and cook for a further 5 minutes, stirring. Add the chicken, stock and herbs, and season to taste with salt and pepper. Bring to the boil, then lower the heat and simmer for 25 minutes, until the chicken is tender and cooked through. Remove from the heat and leave to cool for 10 minutes.

Transfer the soup to a food processor or blender and process until smooth (you may need to do this in batches). Return the soup to the rinsed-out pan and warm over a low heat for 5 minutes.

Stir in the cream and cook for a further 2 minutes, then remove from the heat and ladle into serving bowls. Garnish with sprigs of thyme and serve immediately.

Chicken Noodle Soup

serves 4

2 skinless, boneless
chicken breasts

1.2 litres/2 pints water or
chicken stock

3 carrots, peeled and cut
into 5-mm/¼-inch slices

85 g/3 oz vermicelli
(or other fine noodles)

salt and pepper

fresh tarragon leaves,
to garnish

Place the chicken breasts in a large saucepan, add the water and bring to a simmer. Cook for 25–30 minutes. Skim any scum from the surface if necessary. Remove the chicken from the stock and keep warm.

Continue to simmer the stock, add the carrots and vermicelli and cook for 4–5 minutes.

Thinly slice or shred the chicken breasts and place in warmed serving dishes.

Season the soup to taste with salt and pepper and pour over the chicken. Serve immediately garnished with the tarragon.

Thai Chicken Soup

serves 4

1 tbsp sesame oil or chilli oil

2 garlic cloves, chopped

2 spring onions, trimmed and sliced

1 leek, trimmed and finely sliced

1 tbsp grated fresh root ginger

1 fresh red chilli, deseeded and finely chopped

350 g/12 oz skinless, boneless chicken breasts, cut into strips

850 ml/1½ pints chicken stock

2 tbsp rice wine

1 tbsp chopped lemon grass

6 kaffir lime leaves, finely shredded

200 g/7 oz fine egg noodles

salt and pepper

Heat the oil in a wok or large saucepan. Add the garlic and cook over a medium heat, stirring, for 1 minute, then add the spring onions, leek, ginger and chilli and cook, stirring, for a further 3 minutes. Add the chicken, stock and rice wine, bring to the boil and simmer for 20 minutes. Stir in the lemon grass and kaffir lime leaves.

Bring a separate saucepan of water to the boil and add the noodles. Cook for 3 minutes, drain well, then add them to the soup. Season to taste with salt and pepper. Cook for a further 2 minutes. Remove from the heat, ladle into individual bowls and serve hot.

Chicken & Broccoli Soup

serves 4–6

225 g/8 oz broccoli

55 g/2 oz unsalted butter

1 onion, chopped

25 g/1 oz basmati rice

225 g/8 oz skinless,
boneless chicken breast,
cut into thin slivers

25 g/1 oz plain wholemeal
flour

300 ml/10 fl oz milk

450 ml/16 fl oz chicken
stock

55 g/2 oz sweetcorn kernels

salt and pepper

Break the broccoli into small florets and cook in a saucepan of lightly salted boiling water for 3 minutes, drain, then plunge into cold water and reserve.

Melt the butter in a saucepan over a medium heat, add the onion, rice and chicken and cook for 5 minutes, stirring frequently.

Remove the saucepan from the heat and stir in the flour. Return to the heat and cook for 2 minutes, stirring constantly. Stir in the milk and then the stock. Bring to the boil, stirring constantly, then reduce the heat and simmer for 10 minutes.

Drain the broccoli and add to the saucepan with the sweetcorn and salt and pepper to taste. Simmer for 5 minutes, or until the rice is tender, then serve.

Chicken & Rice Soup

serves 4

1.5 litres/2¾ pints chicken stock

2 small carrots, very thinly sliced

1 celery stick, finely diced

1 baby leek, halved lengthways and thinly sliced

115 g/4 oz petit pois, defrosted if frozen

175 g/6 oz cooked rice

150 g/5½ oz cooked chicken, sliced

2 tsp chopped fresh tarragon

1 tbsp chopped fresh parsley

salt and pepper

sprigs of fresh parsley, to garnish

Put the stock in a large saucepan and add the carrots, celery and leek. Bring to the boil, reduce the heat to low and simmer gently, partially covered, for 10 minutes.

Stir in the petit pois, rice and chicken and continue cooking for a further 10–15 minutes, or until the vegetables are tender.

Add the chopped tarragon and parsley, then taste and adjust the seasoning, adding salt and pepper as needed.

Ladle the soup into warmed bowls, garnish with sprigs of parsley and serve immediately.

Chicken & Potato Soup with Bacon

serves 4

1 tbsp butter

2 garlic cloves, chopped

1 onion, sliced

250 g/9 oz smoked lean back bacon, chopped

2 large leeks, sliced

2 tbsp plain flour

1 litre/1¾ pints chicken stock

800 g/1 lb 12 oz potatoes, chopped

200 g/7 oz skinless, boneless chicken breast, chopped

4 tbsp double cream

salt and pepper

grilled bacon, to garnish

Melt the butter in a large saucepan over a medium heat. Add the garlic and onion and cook, stirring, for 3 minutes, until slightly softened. Add the chopped bacon and leeks and cook for a further 3 minutes, stirring.

In a bowl, mix the flour with enough stock to make a smooth paste, then stir it into the pan. Cook, stirring, for 2 minutes. Pour in the remaining stock, then add the potatoes and chicken. Season to taste with salt and pepper. Bring to the boil, then lower the heat and simmer for 25 minutes, until the chicken and potatoes are tender and cooked through.

Stir in the cream and cook for a further 2 minutes, then remove from the heat and ladle into serving bowls. Garnish with grilled bacon and serve immediately.

Chicken Liver Pâté

serves 4–6

200 g/7 oz butter

225 g/8 oz trimmed chicken livers, thawed if frozen

2 tbsp Marsala or brandy

1½ tsp chopped fresh sage

1 garlic clove, coarsely chopped

150 ml/5 fl oz double cream

salt and pepper

fresh bay leaves or sage leaves, to garnish

crackers, to serve

Melt 40 g/1½ oz of the butter in a large, heavy-based frying pan. Add the chicken livers and cook over a medium heat for about 4 minutes on each side. They should be browned on the outside but still pink in the middle. Transfer to a food processor and process until finely chopped.

Stir the Marsala into the pan, scraping up any sediment with a wooden spoon, then add to the food processor with the chopped sage, garlic and 100 g/3½ oz of the remaining butter. Process until smooth. Add the cream, season to taste with salt and pepper and process until thoroughly combined and smooth. Spoon the pâté into a dish or individual ramekins, smooth the surface and leave to cool completely.

Melt the remaining butter, then spoon it over the surface of the pâté. Decorate with bay leaves, cool, then chill in the refrigerator. Serve with crackers.

Chicken Satay

serves 4

4 tbsp smooth peanut
butter

100 ml/3½ fl oz soy sauce

4 skinless, boneless
chicken breasts, cut into
thin strips

freshly cooked rice,
to serve

lemon wedges, to garnish

If you are using wooden skewers, soak them in cold water for 30 minutes. Preheat the grill. Mix the peanut butter and soy sauce together in a bowl until smooth. Stir in the chicken strips, tossing well to coat in the mixture.

Thread the chicken strips onto 4 metal kebab skewers or pre-soaked wooden skewers and grill for about 5 minutes on each side until cooked through. Serve immediately with rice and garnish with lemon wedges.

Chicken Balls with Dipping Sauce

serves 4

2 large skinless, boneless chicken breasts

3 tbsp vegetable oil

2 shallots, finely chopped

½ celery stick, finely chopped

1 garlic clove, crushed

2 tbsp light soy sauce

1 small egg

1 bunch of spring onions

salt and pepper

for the dipping sauce

3 tbsp dark soy sauce

1 tbsp rice wine

1 tsp sesame seeds

Cut the chicken into 2-cm/¾-inch pieces. Heat half of the oil in a frying pan or wok and stir-fry the chicken over a high heat for 2–3 minutes until golden. Remove from the pan or wok with a draining spoon and set aside.

Add the shallots, celery and garlic to the pan or wok and stir-fry for 1–2 minutes until softened.

Place the chicken, shallots, celery and garlic in a food processor and process until finely minced. Add 1 tablespoon of the light soy sauce and just enough egg to make a fairly firm mixture. Season to taste with salt and pepper.

Trim the spring onions and cut into 5-cm/2-inch lengths. Make the dipping sauce by mixing together the dark soy sauce, rice wine and sesame seeds in a small serving bowl and set aside.

Shape the chicken mixture into 16–18 walnut-sized balls. Heat the remaining oil in the frying pan or wok and stir-fry the chicken balls in small batches for 4–5 minutes until golden brown. As each batch is cooked drain on kitchen paper and keep hot.

Add the spring onions to the pan or wok and stir-fry for 1–2 minutes until they begin to soften, then stir in the remaining light soy sauce. Serve the chicken balls with the stir-fried spring onions and the bowl of dipping sauce.

Sesame Chicken Wings

makes 24

4 tbsp olive oil, plus extra for oiling

finely grated rind and juice of 2 lemons

1 tbsp soft light brown sugar

pinch of cayenne pepper, or to taste

24 chicken wings, any small hairs removed and the thin tips cut off

2 tbsp sesame seeds

salt and pepper

Preheat the oven to 200°C/400°F/Gas Mark 6 and line a roasting tin with foil. Put a grill rack in the tin.

Put the oil in a bowl, add the lemon rind and juice, sugar, cayenne pepper and salt and pepper to taste and stir until the sugar has dissolved. Add the chicken wings and use your hands to coat well with the marinade. At this point, you can cook the wings immediately or cover and leave to marinate in the refrigerator for several hours.

Generously brush the grill rack with oil. Arrange the wings on the rack in a single layer and sprinkle with the sesame seeds. If your grill rack isn't large enough to hold all the wings, cook in batches. Roast in the preheated oven for 25–30 minutes, until the juices run clear when a skewer is inserted into the thickest part of the chicken and the skin is crisp. Transfer to a plate lined with crumpled kitchen paper and leave to cool before serving.

Chicken Crostini

serves 4

12 slices French bread or rustic bread

4 tbsp olive oil

2 garlic cloves, chopped

2 tbsp finely chopped fresh oregano

100 g/3½ oz cold roast chicken, cut into thin slices

4 tomatoes, sliced

12 thin slices of goat's cheese

12 black olives, stoned and chopped

salt and pepper

salad leaves, to serve

Preheat the oven to 180°C/350°F/Gas Mark 4 and the grill to medium. Put the bread under the preheated grill and lightly toast on both sides. Meanwhile, pour the olive oil into a bowl and add the garlic and oregano. Season to taste with salt and pepper and mix well. Remove the toasted bread slices from the grill and brush them on one side only with the oil mixture.

Place the bread slices, oiled sides up, on a baking sheet. Put some sliced chicken on top of each one, followed by a slice of tomato. Divide the slices of goat's cheese between them, then top with the chopped olives. Drizzle over the remaining oil mixture and transfer to the preheated oven. Bake for about 5 minutes, or until the cheese is golden and starting to melt. Remove from the oven and serve with salad leaves.

Coronation Chicken

serves 6

4 tbsp olive oil

900 g/2 lb skinless, boneless chicken, diced

125 g/4½ oz rindless smoked bacon, diced

12 shallots

2 garlic cloves, crushed

1 tbsp mild curry powder

300 ml/10 fl oz mayonnaise

1 tbsp clear honey

1 tbsp chopped fresh parsley

pepper

85 g/3 oz seedless white grapes, quartered, to garnish

cold saffron rice, to serve

Heat the oil in a large, heavy-based frying pan. Add the chicken, bacon, shallots, garlic and curry powder. Cook slowly, stirring, for about 15 minutes.

Spoon the mixture into a clean mixing bowl. Leave to cool completely, then season to taste with pepper.

Blend the mayonnaise with the honey, then add the parsley. Toss the chicken mixture in the mayonnaise mixture.

Place the chicken mixture in a serving dish, garnish with the grapes and serve with cold saffron rice.

Chicken Livers in Red Wine & Thyme

serves 4

250 g/9 oz fresh chicken livers

3 tbsp lemon-flavoured oil

2 garlic cloves, finely chopped

4 tbsp red wine

1 tbsp chopped fresh thyme

salt and pepper

rocket leaves, to serve

sprigs of fresh thyme, to garnish

Rinse the chicken livers under cold running water and pat dry with kitchen paper. Heat the lemon-flavoured oil in a frying pan. Add the garlic and cook, stirring, over a medium heat for 2 minutes. Add the chicken livers, wine and chopped thyme. Season to taste with salt and pepper and cook for 3 minutes.

Meanwhile, arrange the rocket leaves on a large serving platter. Remove the pan from the heat and spoon the chicken livers over the bed of rocket. Pour over the cooking juices, then garnish with sprigs of fresh thyme and serve immediately.

Chicken, Cheese & Rocket Salad

serves 4

150 g/5½ oz rocket leaves

2 celery sticks, trimmed and sliced

½ cucumber, sliced

2 spring onions, trimmed and sliced

2 tbsp chopped fresh parsley

25 g/1 oz walnut pieces

350 g/12 oz boneless roast chicken, sliced

125 g/4½ oz Stilton cheese, cubed

handful of seedless red grapes, halved (optional)

salt and pepper

for the dressing

2 tbsp olive oil

1 tbsp sherry vinegar

1 tsp Dijon mustard

1 tbsp chopped fresh mixed herbs

Wash the rocket leaves, pat dry with kitchen paper and put them into a large salad bowl. Add the celery, cucumber, spring onions, parsley and walnuts and mix together well. Transfer to a large serving platter. Arrange the chicken slices over the salad, then scatter over the Stilton cheese. Add the grapes, if using. Season well with salt and pepper.

To make the dressing, put all the ingredients into a screw-top jar and shake well. Alternatively, put them into a bowl and mix together well. Drizzle the dressing over the salad and serve.

Smoked Chicken & Cranberry Salad

serves 4

1 smoked chicken,
weighing 1.3 kg/3 lb

115 g/4 oz dried cranberries

2 tbsp apple juice or water

200 g/7 oz sugar snap peas

2 ripe avocados

juice of ½ lemon

4 lettuce hearts

1 bunch of watercress,
trimmed

55 g/2 oz rocket

55 g/2 oz chopped walnuts,
to garnish (optional)

for the dressing

2 tbsp olive oil

1 tbsp walnut oil

2 tbsp lemon juice

1 tbsp chopped fresh mixed
herbs, such as parsley
and lemon thyme

salt and pepper

Carve the chicken carefully, slicing the white meat. Divide the legs into thighs and drumsticks and trim the wings. Cover with clingfilm and refrigerate.

Put the cranberries in a bowl. Stir in the apple juice, cover with clingfilm and leave to soak for 30 minutes.

Meanwhile, blanch the sugar snap peas, refresh under cold running water and drain.

Peel, stone and slice the avocados, then toss in the lemon juice to prevent browning.

Separate the lettuce hearts and arrange on a large serving platter with the avocados, sugar snap peas, watercress, rocket and chicken.

Put all the dressing ingredients, with salt and pepper to taste, into a screw-top jar and shake well.

Drain the cranberries and mix them with the dressing, then pour over the salad.

Serve immediately, scattered with walnuts, if using.

Chicken & Spinach Salad

serves 4

3 celery sticks, thinly sliced

½ cucumber, thinly sliced

2 spring onions, thinly sliced

250 g/9 oz young spinach leaves

3 tbsp chopped fresh parsley

350 g/12 oz cold roast chicken, thinly sliced

smoked almonds, to garnish

for the dressing

2.5-cm/1-inch piece fresh root ginger, finely grated

3 tbsp olive oil

1 tbsp white wine vinegar

1 tbsp clear honey

½ tsp ground cinnamon

salt and pepper

Toss the celery, cucumber and spring onions in a large bowl with the spinach leaves and parsley.

Transfer the salad to serving plates and arrange the chicken on top.

In a screw-top jar, combine all the dressing ingredients, including salt and pepper to taste, and shake well to mix. Pour the dressing over the salad. Garnish with a few smoked almonds.

Waldorf Chicken Salad

serves 4

500 g/1 lb 2 oz red apples, diced

3 tbsp lemon juice

150 ml/5 fl oz mayonnaise

1 head celery

4 shallots, sliced

1 garlic clove, crushed

85 g/3 oz chopped walnuts, plus extra to garnish

500 g/1 lb 2 oz lean cooked chicken, cubed

1 cos lettuce

pepper

Place the apples in a bowl with the lemon juice and 1 tablespoon of the mayonnaise. Leave for 40 minutes or until required.

Slice the celery very thinly. Add the celery with the shallots, garlic and walnuts to the apples, mix and then add the remaining mayonnaise and blend thoroughly.

Add the chicken, season to taste with pepper and mix with the other ingredients.

Line a serving dish with the lettuce. Pile the chicken salad into the dish, garnish with chopped walnuts and serve.

Cajun Chicken Salad

serves 4

4 skinless, boneless chicken breasts, about 140 g/5 oz each

4 tsp Cajun seasoning

2 tsp sunflower oil

1 ripe mango, peeled, stoned and cut into thick slices

200 g/7 oz mixed salad leaves

1 red onion, halved and thinly sliced

175 g/6 oz cooked beetroot, diced

85 g/3 oz radishes, sliced

55 g/2 oz walnut halves

4 tbsp walnut oil

1–2 tsp Dijon mustard

1 tbsp lemon juice

2 tbsp sesame seeds

salt and pepper

Make 3 diagonal slashes across each chicken breast. Put the chicken into a shallow dish and sprinkle all over with the Cajun seasoning. Cover and refrigerate for at least 30 minutes.

When ready to cook, brush a griddle pan with the oil. Heat over a high heat until very hot and a few drops of water sprinkled into the pan sizzle immediately. Add the chicken and cook for 7–8 minutes on each side, or until thoroughly cooked. If still slightly pink in the centre, cook a little longer. Remove the chicken and reserve.

Add the mango slices to the pan and cook for 2 minutes on each side. Remove and reserve.

Meanwhile, arrange the salad leaves in a serving bowl and scatter over the onion, beetroot, radishes and walnut halves.

Put the walnut oil, mustard, lemon juice and salt and pepper to taste in a screw-top jar and shake until well blended. Pour over the salad and sprinkle with the sesame seeds.

Cut the reserved chicken into thick slices. Arrange the chicken and reserved mango slices on top of the salad and serve immediately.

2

Light Bites

Mediterranean Pan Bagna

serves 2

1 garlic clove, halved

1 large baguette, cut lengthways

4 tbsp olive oil

140 g/5 oz cold roast chicken, thinly sliced

2 large tomatoes, sliced

20 g/¾ oz canned anchovy fillets, drained

8 large stoned black olives, chopped

pepper

Rub the garlic over the cut side of the bread and sprinkle with the oil.

Arrange the chicken on top of the bread. Arrange the tomatoes and anchovies on top of the chicken.

Scatter with the black olives and season with plenty of pepper. Sandwich the loaf back together and wrap tightly in foil until required. Cut into slices to serve.

Open Chicken Sandwiches

serves 6

3 hard-boiled eggs, the yolk mashed and the white chopped

25 g/1 oz butter, softened

2 tbsp English mustard

1 tsp anchovy essence

250 g/9 oz Cheddar cheese, grated

3 cooked skinless, boneless chicken breasts, diced

6 thick slices of rustic bread, buttered

12 slices each of tomato and cucumber

pepper

In a large bowl, mix the egg yolks and whites with the softened butter, English mustard and anchovy essence and season to taste with pepper.

Mix in the Cheddar and chicken and spread the mixture on the bread.

Arrange the tomato and cucumber slices on top of the egg and serve.

Smoked Chicken & Ham Focaccia

serves 2–4

1 thick focaccia loaf (about 15–17.5 cm/6–7 inches

handful of basil leaves

2 small courgettes, coarsely grated

6 wafer-thin slices of smoked chicken

6 wafer-thin slices of cooked ham

225 g/8 oz taleggio cheese, cut into strips

freshly grated nutmeg (optional)

cherry tomatoes, to serve

Preheat a griddle plate or pan under the grill until both grill and griddle are hot. If you do not have a griddle, heat a heavy baking sheet or roasting tin instead. Slice the focaccia in half horizontally and cut the top half into strips.

Cover the bottom half of the focaccia (or whole bread) with basil leaves, top with the courgettes in an even layer and then cover with the chicken and ham, alternating the slices and wrinkling them. Lay the strips of focaccia on top, placing strips of taleggio cheese between them. Sprinkle with a little nutmeg, if using.

Place the assembled bread on the hot griddle and cook under the grill, well away from the heat, for about 5 minutes, until the taleggio has melted and the top of the bread is browned. Serve immediately with cherry tomatoes, cutting the bread into four across the strips.

Chicken Wraps

serves 4

150 g/5½ oz natural yogurt

1 tbsp wholegrain mustard

280 g/10 oz cooked skinless, boneless chicken breast, diced

140 g/5 oz iceberg lettuce, finely shredded

85 g/3 oz cucumber, thinly sliced

2 celery sticks, sliced

85 g/3 oz black seedless grapes, halved

8 x 20-cm/8-inch soft flour tortillas or 4 x 25-cm/ 10-inch soft flour tortillas

pepper

Combine the yogurt and mustard in a bowl and season to taste with pepper. Stir in the chicken and toss until thoroughly coated.

Put the lettuce, cucumber, celery and grapes into a separate bowl and mix well.

Fold a tortilla in half and in half again to make a cone that is easy to hold. Half-fill the tortilla pocket with the salad mixture and top with some of the chicken mixture. Repeat with the remaining tortillas, salad and chicken. Serve immediately.

Cheese & Chicken Toasts

serves 4

250 g/9 oz Wensleydale cheese, grated

250 g/9 oz cooked chicken, shredded

25g/1 oz butter

1 tbsp Worcestershire sauce

1 tsp dry English mustard

2 tsp plain flour

4 tbsp mild beer

4 slices of bread

salt and pepper

cherry tomatoes, to serve

Place the Wensleydale cheese, chicken, butter, Worcestershire sauce, mustard, plain flour and beer in a small saucepan. Mix all the ingredients together then season to taste with salt and pepper.

Gently bring the mixture to the boil, then remove from the heat.

Using a wooden spoon, beat the mixture until it becomes creamy in texture. Leave the mixture to cool.

Once the chicken mixture has cooled, toast the bread on both sides and spread with the chicken mixture.

Place under a hot grill and cook until bubbling and golden brown. Serve immediately with the cherry tomatoes.

Spicy Chicken Muffins

makes 12

125 ml/4 fl oz vegetable oil, plus extra for greasing

2 onions, chopped

3 spring onions, chopped

1 fresh red chilli, deseeded and finely chopped

3 skinless, boneless chicken thighs, chopped

1 tsp paprika

315 g/11 oz self-raising flour

1 tsp baking powder

2 eggs

1 tbsp lemon juice

1 tbsp grated lemon rind

125 ml/4 fl oz soured cream

125 ml/4 fl oz natural yogurt

Preheat the oven to 190°C/375°F/Gas Mark 5. Grease a 12-cup muffin tin with oil. Heat a little of the oil in a frying pan, add the onions, spring onions and chilli and cook over a low heat, stirring constantly, for 3 minutes. Remove from the heat, lift out the onions and chilli and set aside. Heat a little more oil in the frying pan, add the chicken and paprika, and cook, stirring, over a medium heat for 5 minutes. Remove from the heat and set aside.

Sift the flour and baking powder into a large mixing bowl. In a separate bowl, lightly beat the eggs, then stir in the remaining oil and the lemon juice and rind. Pour in the soured cream and the yogurt and mix together. Add the egg mixture to the flour mixture, then gently stir in the onions, spring onions, chilli and chicken. Do not over-stir the mixture — it is fine for it to be a little lumpy.

Divide the muffin mixture evenly between the 12 cups in the muffin tin (they should be about two-thirds full), then transfer to the oven. Bake in the preheated oven for about 20 minutes, or until risen and golden. Remove the muffins from the oven and serve warm, or put them on a wire rack and leave to cool.

Chicken Fajitas

serves 4

3 tbsp olive oil, plus extra
for drizzling

3 tbsp maple syrup or clear
honey

1 tbsp red wine vinegar

2 garlic cloves, crushed

2 tsp dried oregano

1–2 tsp dried chilli flakes

4 skinless, boneless
chicken breasts

2 red peppers, deseeded
and cut into 2.5-cm/
1-inch strips

salt and pepper

warmed flour tortillas and
shredded lettuce,
to serve

Place the oil, maple syrup, vinegar, garlic, oregano, chilli flakes and salt and pepper to taste in a large, shallow dish or bowl and mix together.

Slice the chicken across the grain into slices 2.5 cm/1 inch thick. Toss in the marinade until well coated. Cover and leave to chill in the refrigerator for 2–3 hours, turning occasionally.

Heat a griddle pan until hot. Lift the chicken slices from the marinade with a slotted spoon, lay on the griddle pan and cook over a medium-high heat for 3–4 minutes on each side, or until cooked through. Remove the chicken to a warmed plate and keep warm.

Add the peppers, skin side down, to the griddle pan and cook for 2 minutes on each side. Transfer to the plate.

Divide the chicken and peppers between the flour tortillas, top with a little shredded lettuce, wrap and serve immediately.

Chicken & Chilli Enchiladas

serves 4

corn oil, for brushing

5 fresh hot green chillies, such as jalapeño, deseeded and chopped

1 Spanish onion, chopped

2 garlic cloves, chopped

2 tbsp chopped fresh coriander

2 tbsp lime juice

125 ml/4 fl oz chicken stock

2 beef tomatoes, peeled, deseeded and chopped

pinch of sugar

350 g/12 oz cooked chicken, shredded

85 g/3 oz queso anejo or Cheddar cheese, grated

2 tsp chopped fresh oregano

8 corn or flour tortillas

salt

Preheat the oven to 180°C/350°F/Gas Mark 4 and brush a large, ovenproof dish with oil. Place two-thirds of the chillies, the onion, garlic, coriander, lime juice, stock, tomatoes and sugar in a food processor and pulse to a purée. Scrape into a saucepan and simmer over a medium heat for 10 minutes, until thickened.

Mix the remaining chillies, the chicken, 55 g/2 oz of the cheese and the oregano together. Season with salt and stir in half the sauce.

Heat the tortillas in a dry, heavy-based frying pan or in the microwave according to the packet instructions. Divide the chicken mixture between them, spooning it along the centres, then roll up and place, seam-side down, in the dish.

Pour the remaining sauce over the enchiladas and sprinkle with the remaining cheese. Bake in the preheated oven for 20 minutes and serve hot.

The Ultimate Chicken Burger

serves 4

4 large skinless, boneless chicken breasts

1 large egg white

1 tbsp cornflour

1 tbsp plain flour

1 egg, beaten

55 g/2 oz fresh white breadcrumbs

2 tbsp sunflower oil

2 beef tomatoes, sliced

to serve

4 burger buns, sliced

shredded lettuce

mayonnaise

Place the chicken breasts between 2 sheets of non-stick baking parchment and flatten slightly using a meat mallet or a rolling pin. Beat the egg white and cornflour together, then brush over the chicken. Cover and leave to chill for 30 minutes, then coat in the flour.

Place the egg and breadcrumbs in 2 separate bowls and coat the burgers first in the egg, allowing any excess to drip back into the bowl, then in the breadcrumbs.

Heat a heavy-based frying pan and add the oil. When hot, add the burgers and cook over a medium heat for 6–8 minutes on each side, or until thoroughly cooked. Add the tomato slices for the last 1–2 minutes of the cooking time to heat through.

Serve the burgers in the burger buns with the tomato slices, a little shredded lettuce and a spoonful of mayonnaise.

Bacon-wrapped Chicken Burgers

serves 4

450 g/1 lb fresh chicken mince

1 onion, grated

2 garlic cloves, crushed

55 g/2 oz pine kernels, toasted

55 g/2 oz Gruyère cheese, grated

2 tbsp fresh snipped chives

2 tbsp wholemeal flour

8 slices lean back bacon

1–2 tbsp sunflower oil

salt and pepper

to serve

4 crusty rolls, sliced

sliced red onion

chopped lettuce

mayonnaise

chopped spring onions

Place the chicken mince, onion, garlic, pine kernels, Gruyère cheese, chives and salt and pepper in a food processor. Using the pulse button, blend the mixture together using short sharp bursts. Scrape out onto a board and shape into 4 even-sized burgers. Coat in the flour, then cover and chill for 1 hour.

Wrap each burger with 2 bacon slices, securing in place with a wooden cocktail stick.

Heat a heavy-based frying pan and add the oil. When hot, add the burgers and cook over a medium heat for 5–6 minutes on each side, or until thoroughly cooked through.

Serve the burgers in the crusty rolls with sliced red onion, chopped lettuce, a spoonful of mayonnaise and chopped spring onions.

Chicken & Herb Fritters

makes 8

500 g/1 lb 2 oz mashed potato, with butter added

250 g/9 oz cooked chicken, chopped

125 g/4½ oz cooked ham, finely chopped

1 tbsp fresh mixed herbs

2 eggs, lightly beaten

1 tbsp milk

125 g/4½ oz fresh wholemeal breadcrumbs

oil, for shallow-frying

salt and pepper

mixed salad, to serve

In a large bowl, blend the potatoes, chicken, ham, herbs and 1 of the eggs, and season to taste with salt and pepper. Shape the mixture into small balls or flat pancakes.

Place the remaining egg in a shallow dish and stir in the milk.

Place the breadcrumbs on a plate. Dip the balls in the egg and milk mixture, then roll in the breadcrumbs to coat them completely.

Heat the oil in a large, heavy-based frying pan and cook the fritters until they are golden brown. Serve hot with a mixed salad.

Baked Potatoes with Chicken

serves 4

4 large baking potatoes, pricked with a fork

250 g/9 oz cooked chicken, diced

4 spring onions, thickly sliced

250 g/9 oz low-fat soft cheese

pepper

mixed salad, to serve

Preheat the oven to 200°C/400°F/Gas Mark 6. Bake the potatoes in the preheated oven for about 60 minutes, until tender, or cook in a microwave on high power for 12–15 minutes.

Mix the chicken and spring onions with the low-fat soft cheese.

Cut a cross through the top of each potato and squeeze slightly apart. Spoon the chicken filling into the potatoes and season to taste with pepper. Serve with a mixed salad.

Chicken Kebabs in a Yogurt Marinade

serves 4

300 ml/10 fl oz
Greek yogurt

2 garlic cloves, crushed

juice of ½ lemon

1 tbsp chopped fresh herbs
such as oregano, dill,
tarragon or parsley

4 large skinless, boneless
chicken breasts

salt and pepper

to serve

freshly cooked rice

shredded lettuce

lemon wedges

To make the sauce, put the yogurt, garlic, lemon juice, herbs, and salt and pepper to taste in a large bowl and mix well together.

Cut the chicken breasts into chunks measuring about 4 cm/ 1¹/₂ inches square. Add to the yogurt mixture and toss well together until the chicken pieces are coated. Cover and leave to marinate in the refrigerator for about 1 hour. If you are using wooden skewers, soak them in cold water for 30 minutes.

Preheat the grill. Thread the pieces of chicken onto 8 metal kebab skewers or pre-soaked wooden skewers and place on a grill pan.

Cook the kebabs under the preheated grill for about 15 minutes, turning and basting occasionally with the remaining marinade, until lightly browned and tender. Serve the kebabs on a bed of rice and shredded lettuce with lemon wedges for squeezing over.

Chicken & Tomato Skewers

serves 4

500 g/1 lb 2 oz skinless, boneless chicken breasts

3 tbsp tomato purée

2 tbsp clear honey

2 tbsp Worcestershire sauce

1 tbsp chopped fresh rosemary

250 g/9 oz cherry tomatoes

couscous or rice, to serve

sprigs of fresh rosemary, to garnish

If you are using wooden skewers, soak them in cold water for 30 minutes. Cut the chicken into 2.5-cm/1-inch chunks and place in a bowl.

Combine the tomato purée, honey, Worcestershire sauce and chopped rosemary in a small bowl. Add to the chicken, stirring to coat evenly.

Preheat the grill. Alternating the chicken pieces and cherry tomatoes, thread them onto 8 metal kebab skewers or pre-soaked wooden skewers.

Spoon over any remaining glaze. Cook under the preheated grill for about 8–10 minutes, turning occasionally, until the chicken is thoroughly cooked.

Serve with couscous or rice and garnish with sprigs of rosemary.

Skewered Chicken Spirals

serves 4

4 skinless, boneless chicken breasts

1 garlic clove, crushed

2 tbsp tomato purée

4 slices smoked back bacon

large handful of fresh basil leaves

vegetable oil, for brushing

salt and pepper

mixed salad, to serve

If you are using wooden skewers, soak them in cold water for 30 minutes. Spread out a piece of chicken between two sheets of clingfilm and beat firmly with a rolling pin or meat mallet to flatten the chicken to an even thickness. Repeat with the remaining chicken breasts.

Combine the garlic and tomato purée and spread the mixture over the chicken. Lay a bacon slice over each, then sprinkle with the basil. Season to taste with salt and pepper.

Roll up each piece of chicken firmly, then cut into thick slices. Thread the slices onto 4 metal kebab skewers or pre-soaked wooden skewers, making sure the skewer holds the chicken in a spiral shape.

Brush lightly with oil and cook under a preheated grill for about 10 minutes, turning once. Serve hot with a mixed salad.

Fettuccine with Chicken & Basil Pesto

serves 4

2 tbsp vegetable oil

4 skinless, boneless chicken breasts

350 g/12 oz dried fettuccine

salt and pepper

sprig of fresh basil, to garnish

for the pesto

100 g/3½ oz shredded fresh basil

125 ml/4 fl oz extra virgin olive oil

3 tbsp pine kernels

3 garlic cloves, crushed

55 g/2 oz freshly grated Parmesan cheese

2 tbsp freshly grated pecorino cheese

salt

To make the pesto, put the basil, olive oil, pine kernels, garlic and a generous pinch of salt in a food processor or blender. Process the ingredients until smooth. Scrape the mixture into a bowl and stir in the cheeses.

Heat the vegetable oil in a frying pan over a medium heat. Cook the chicken breasts, turning once, for 8–10 minutes, until the juices are no longer pink. Cut into small cubes.

Meanwhile, bring a large saucepan of lightly salted water to the boil. Add the pasta, bring back to the boil and cook for 8–10 minutes, or until tender but still firm to the bite. Drain and transfer to a warmed serving dish. Add the chicken and pesto, then season to taste with pepper. Toss well to mix.

Garnish with a sprig of basil and serve warm.

Five-spice Chicken with Vegetables

serves 4

2 tbsp sesame oil

1 garlic clove, chopped

3 spring onions, trimmed and sliced

1 tbsp cornflour

2 tbsp rice wine

4 skinless, boneless chicken breasts, cut into strips

1 tbsp Chinese five-spice powder

1 tbsp grated fresh root ginger

125 ml/4 fl oz chicken stock

100 g/3½ oz baby corn cobs, sliced

300 g/10½ oz beansprouts

finely chopped spring onion, to garnish (optional)

freshly cooked jasmine rice, to serve

Heat the oil in a preheated wok or large frying pan. Add the garlic and the sliced spring onions and stir-fry over a medium-high heat for 1 minute.

In a bowl, mix together the cornflour and rice wine, then add the mixture to the pan. Stir-fry for 1 minute, then add the chicken, five-spice powder, ginger and stock and cook for a further 4 minutes. Add the corn cobs and cook for 2 minutes, then add the beansprouts and cook for a further minute.

Remove from the heat, garnish with chopped spring onions, if using, and serve with freshly cooked jasmine rice.

Chicken & Peanut Stir-fry

serves 4

2 tbsp groundnut oil

1 garlic clove, chopped

3 spring onions, trimmed and sliced

4 skinless, boneless chicken breasts, cut into bite-sized chunks

1 tbsp grated fresh root ginger

½ tsp chilli powder

150 g/5½ oz sugar snap peas, trimmed

125 g/4½ oz baby corn cobs

2 tbsp smooth peanut butter

1 tbsp light soy sauce

freshly cooked rice, to serve

Heat the oil in a preheated wok or large frying pan. Add the garlic and spring onions and stir-fry over a medium-high heat for 1 minute. Add the chicken, ginger and chilli powder and stir-fry for a further 4 minutes. Add the sugar snap peas and baby corn cobs and cook for 2 minutes.

In a bowl, mix together the peanut butter and soy sauce, then add it to the wok. Stir-fry for a further minute.

Remove from the heat, pile onto 4 serving dishes and serve with freshly cooked rice.

Main
Courses

Chicken, Potato & Leek Pie

serves 4

225 g/8 oz waxy potatoes, cubed

5 tbsp butter

1 skinless, boneless chicken breast, about 175 g/6 oz, cubed

1 leek, sliced

150 g/5½ oz chestnut mushrooms, sliced

2½ tbsp plain flour

300 ml/10 fl oz milk

1 tbsp Dijon mustard

2 tbsp chopped fresh sage

225 g/8 oz filo pastry, thawed if frozen

3 tbsp melted butter

salt and pepper

Preheat the oven to 180°C/350°F/Gas Mark 4. Cook the potato cubes in a saucepan of boiling water for 5 minutes. Drain and set aside.

Melt the butter in a frying pan and cook the chicken cubes for 5 minutes or until browned all over.

Add the leek and mushrooms and cook for 3 minutes, stirring. Stir in the flour and cook for 1 minute stirring constantly. Gradually stir in the milk and bring to the boil. Add the mustard, sage and reserved potato cubes and simmer for 10 minutes. Season to taste with salt and pepper.

Meanwhile, line a deep pie dish with half of the filo pastry. Spoon the filling into the dish and cover with 1 sheet of pastry. Brush the pastry with butter and lay another sheet on top. Brush this sheet with butter.

Cut the remaining filo pastry into strips and fold them onto the top of the pie to create a ruffled effect. Brush the strips with the melted butter and cook in the preheated oven for 45 minutes or until golden brown and crisp. Serve hot.

Chicken Nuggets

serves 4

3 skinless, boneless
chicken breasts

4 tbsp wholemeal plain
flour

1 tbsp wheatgerm

½ tsp ground cumin

½ tsp ground coriander

1 egg, lightly beaten

2 tbsp olive oil

100 g/3½ oz sunblush
tomatoes

100 g/3½ oz fresh
tomatoes, peeled,
deseeded and chopped

2 tbsp mayonnaise

pepper

Preheat the oven to 190°C/375°F/Gas Mark 5. Cut the chicken breasts into 4-cm/1½-inch chunks. Mix the flour, wheatgerm, cumin, coriander, and pepper to taste, in a bowl, then divide in half and put on 2 separate plates. Put the beaten egg on a third plate.

Pour the oil into a baking tray and heat in the oven. Roll the chicken pieces in one plate of flour, shake to remove any excess, then roll in the egg and in the second plate of flour, again shaking off any excess flour. When all the nuggets are ready, remove the baking tray from the oven and toss the nuggets in the hot oil. Roast in the oven for 25–30 minutes until golden and crisp.

Meanwhile, to make the dipping sauce, put both kinds of tomatoes in a blender or food processor and process until smooth. Add the mayonnaise and process again until well combined.

Remove the nuggets from the oven and drain on kitchen paper. Serve with the dipping sauce.

Cheddar-baked Chicken

serves 4

1 tbsp milk

2 tbsp English mustard

55 g/2 oz mature Cheddar cheese, grated

3 tbsp plain flour

2 tbsp snipped fresh chives

4 skinless, boneless chicken breasts

salad leaves, to serve

Preheat the oven to 200°C/400°F/Gas Mark 6. Mix together the milk and mustard in a bowl. In another bowl, combine the cheese, flour and chives.

Dip the chicken into the milk and mustard mixture, brushing to coat evenly.

Dip the chicken breasts into the cheese mixture, pressing to coat evenly. Place on a baking tray and spoon any spare cheese coating over the top.

Bake in the preheated oven for 30–35 minutes, until golden brown and the juices run clear when a skewer is inserted into the thickest part of the meat. Serve the chicken hot with salad leaves.

Crispy-coated Chicken Breasts

serves 4

for the sweet potato wedges

4 large sweet potatoes, peeled and cut into wedges

4 tbsp vegetable oil

1 tsp chilli powder

for the crispy-coated chicken

50 g/1¾ oz hazelnuts, toasted and ground

25 g/1 oz dried white or wholemeal breadcrumbs

2 tbsp freshly grated pecorino cheese

1 tbsp chopped fresh parsley

4 skinless, boneless chicken breasts

1 egg, beaten

4 tbsp vegetable oil

salt and pepper

sprigs of fresh parsley, to garnish

lemon wedges, to serve

Preheat the oven to 200°C/400°F/Gas Mark 6. To make the potato wedges, bring a large saucepan of water to the boil. Add the potatoes, cook over a medium heat for 5 minutes, then drain. Pour 2 tablespoons of the oil into a bowl and stir in the chilli powder. Add the potatoes and turn in the mixture until coated. Transfer to a baking sheet, drizzle over the remaining oil and bake for 35–40 minutes, turning frequently, until golden and cooked through.

About 15 minutes before the end of the cooking time, put the hazelnuts, breadcrumbs, cheese and parsley into a bowl, season to taste with salt and pepper and mix. Dip the chicken breasts into the egg, then coat in the breadcrumb mixture.

Heat the oil in a frying pan. Add the chicken and cook over a medium heat for 3–4 minutes on each side until golden. Lift out and drain on kitchen paper.

Remove the potatoes from the oven, divide between 4 serving plates and add a chicken breast to each. Garnish with parsley and serve with lemon wedges.

Chicken Tikka Masala

serves 4–6

30 g/1 oz ghee or
2 tbsp vegetable or
groundnut oil

1 large garlic clove, finely
chopped

1 fresh red chilli, deseeded
and chopped

2 tsp ground cumin

2 tsp paprika

½ tsp salt

400 g/14 oz canned
chopped tomatoes

300 ml/10 fl oz double
cream

8 pieces cooked tandoori
chicken

pepper

sprigs of fresh coriander,
to garnish

freshly cooked rice,
to serve

To make the tikka masala, heat the ghee in a large frying pan with a lid over a medium heat. Add the garlic and chilli and stir-fry for 1 minute. Stir in the cumin, paprika, salt and pepper to taste and continue stirring for about 30 seconds.

Stir the tomatoes with their juices and the cream into the pan. Reduce the heat to low and leave the sauce to simmer for about 10 minutes, stirring frequently, until it reduces and thickens.

Meanwhile, remove all the bones and any skin from the tandoori chicken pieces, then cut the meat into bite-sized pieces.

Add the chicken pieces to the pan, cover and leave to simmer for 3–5 minutes, until the chicken is heated through. Sprinkle with the sprigs of coriander and serve with freshly cooked rice.

Chicken Pepperonata

serves 4

8 skinless chicken thighs

2 tbsp wholemeal flour

2 tbsp olive oil

1 small onion, thinly sliced

1 garlic clove, crushed

1 each large red, yellow and green peppers, deseeded and thinly sliced

400 g/14 oz canned chopped tomatoes

1 tbsp chopped fresh oregano, plus extra to garnish

salt and pepper

crusty wholemeal bread, to serve

Toss the chicken thighs in the flour, shaking off the excess.

Heat the oil in a wide frying pan and cook the chicken quickly until sealed and lightly browned, then remove from the pan.

Add the onion to the pan and cook gently until soft. Add the garlic, peppers, tomatoes and oregano, then bring to the boil, stirring.

Arrange the chicken over the vegetables, season well with salt and pepper, then cover the pan tightly and simmer for 20 25 minutes or until the chicken is completely cooked and tender.

Taste and adjust the seasoning, if necessary, garnish with oregano and serve with crusty wholemeal bread.

Mexican Drumsticks

serves 4

2 tbsp oil

8 chicken drumsticks

1 onion, finely chopped

1 tsp chilli powder

1 tsp ground coriander

400 g/14 oz canned chopped tomatoes

2 tbsp tomato purée

125 g/4½ oz frozen sweetcorn

salt and pepper

mixed pepper salad, to serve

Heat the oil in a large, heavy-based frying pan, add the chicken drumsticks and cook over a medium heat until lightly browned. Remove from the pan with a slotted spoon and set aside until required.

Add the onion to the pan and cook for 3–4 minutes, until softened, then stir in the chilli powder and coriander and cook for a few seconds, stirring briskly so the spices do not burn. Add the tomatoes and the tomato purée and stir well to combine.

Return the chicken drumsticks to the pan and simmer gently for 20 minutes, until the chicken is tender and thoroughly cooked. Add the sweetcorn and cook for a further 3–4 minutes. Season to taste with salt and pepper.

Serve hot with a mixed pepper salad.

Roasted Chicken & Sweet Potatoes

serves 4

8 chicken thighs

1 red onion, finely chopped

8 tbsp tomato ketchup

2 tbsp maple syrup

1 tbsp Worcestershire sauce

1 tbsp coarse-grain mustard

1 garlic clove, finely chopped

3 tbsp olive oil

4 sweet potatoes, peeled and cut into chunks

Preheat the oven to 200°C/400°F/Gas Mark 6. Score each chicken thigh 2–3 times.

Mix all the remaining ingredients, except the sweet potatoes, together in a large bowl. Add the chicken and toss well to coat. Cover with clingfilm and leave to marinate in a cool place for 20 minutes, then add the sweet potatoes and toss well to coat.

Tip the chicken and sweet potatoes into a baking dish and roast in the preheated oven for 40–50 minutes until well browned. The chicken should be tender and the juices run clear when a skewer is inserted into the thickest part of the meat.

Serve immediately.

Thai Chicken

serves 4

6 garlic cloves, coarsely chopped

1 tsp black pepper

8 chicken legs

1 tbsp Thai fish sauce

4 tbsp dark soy sauce

fresh root ginger, cut into matchsticks, to garnish

Put the garlic cloves in a mortar, add the pepper and pound to a paste with a pestle. Using a sharp knife, make 3–4 diagonal slashes on both sides of the chicken legs. Spread the garlic paste over the chicken legs and place them in a dish. Add the fish sauce and soy sauce and turn the chicken to coat well. Cover with clingfilm and leave to marinate in the refrigerator for 2 hours.

Preheat the grill. Drain the chicken legs, reserving the marinade. Put them on a grill rack and cook under the grill, turning and basting frequently with the reserved marinade, for 20–25 minutes, or until cooked through and tender. The juices should run clear when a skewer is inserted into the thickest part of the meat. Serve immediately garnished with the ginger.

Grilled Chicken with Lemon

serves 4

4 chicken quarters

grated rind and juice of
2 lemons

4 tbsp olive oil

2 garlic cloves, crushed

2 sprigs of fresh thyme,
plus extra to garnish

salt and pepper

Prick the skin of the chicken quarters all over with a fork.
Put the chicken pieces in a dish, add the lemon juice, oil,
garlic, thyme, and salt and pepper to taste and mix well.
Cover and leave to marinate in the fridge for at least
2 hours.

To cook the chicken, preheat the grill. Put the chicken
in a grill pan and baste with the marinade. Cook for
30–40 minutes, basting and turning occasionally, until the
chicken is tender. The juices should run clear when a skewer
is inserted into the thickest part of the meat. Serve hot
garnished with the grated lemon rind and sprigs of thyme.

Jerk Chicken

serves 4

2 fresh red chillies

2 tbsp corn oil, plus extra for brushing

2 garlic cloves, finely chopped

1 tbsp finely chopped onion

1 tbsp finely chopped spring onion

1 tbsp white wine vinegar

1 tbsp lime juice

2 tsp demerara sugar

1 tsp dried thyme

1 tsp ground cinnamon

1 tsp ground mixed spice

¼ tsp freshly grated nutmeg

4 chicken quarters

salt and pepper

sprigs of fresh coriander and lime wedges, to garnish

Deseed and finely chop the red chillies, then place them in a small glass bowl with the oil, garlic, onion, spring onion, vinegar, lime juice, sugar, thyme, cinnamon, mixed spice and nutmeg. Season to taste with salt and pepper and mash thoroughly with a fork.

Using a sharp knife, make a series of diagonal slashes in the chicken pieces and place them in a large, shallow, non-metallic dish. Spoon the jerk seasoning over the chicken, rubbing it well into the slashes. Cover and leave to marinate in the refrigerator for up to 8 hours.

Preheat the grill. Remove the chicken from the marinade, discarding the marinade, brush with oil and cook under the preheated grill, turning frequently, for 30–35 minutes. Transfer to plates and serve garnished with sprigs of coriander and lime wedges.

Mustard & Honey Drumsticks

serves 4

8 chicken drumsticks

sprigs of fresh parsley, to garnish

for the glaze

125 ml/4 fl oz clear honey

4 tbsp Dijon mustard

4 tbsp wholegrain mustard

4 tbsp white wine vinegar

2 tbsp sunflower oil

salt and pepper

Using a sharp knife, make 2–3 diagonal slashes in the chicken drumsticks and place them in a large, non-metallic dish.

Mix all the ingredients for the glaze together in a jug and season to taste with salt and pepper. Pour the glaze over the drumsticks, turning until the drumsticks are well coated. Cover with clingfilm and leave to marinate in the refrigerator for at least 1 hour.

Preheat the grill. Drain the chicken drumsticks, reserving the marinade. Cook the chicken under the preheated grill, turning frequently and brushing with the reserved marinade, for 25–30 minutes, or until thoroughly cooked. Transfer to serving plates, garnish with sprigs of parsley and serve immediately.

Sticky Lime Chicken

serves 4

4 part-boned, skinless chicken breasts, about 140 g/5 oz each

grated rind and juice of 1 lime

1 tbsp clear honey

1 tbsp olive oil

1 garlic clove, chopped (optional)

1 tbsp chopped fresh thyme, plus extra sprigs to garnish

pepper

roasted cherry tomatoes, to serve

Preheat the oven to 190°C/375°F/Gas Mark 5. Arrange the chicken breasts in a shallow roasting tin.

Put the lime rind and juice, honey, oil, garlic, if using, and thyme in a small bowl and combine thoroughly. Spoon the mixture evenly over the chicken breasts and season to taste with pepper.

Roast the chicken in the preheated oven, basting every 10 minutes, for 35–40 minutes, or until the chicken is tender and the juices run clear when a skewer is inserted into the thickest part of the meat. As the chicken cooks the liquid in the pan will thicken to give a sticky coating.

Garnish with sprigs of thyme and serve with roasted cherry tomatoes.

Sweet & Sour Chicken

serves 4

4 skinless, boneless chicken breasts

75 g/2¾ oz plain flour

2 tbsp olive oil

2 large garlic cloves, chopped

1 bay leaf

1 tbsp grated fresh root ginger

1 tbsp chopped fresh lemon grass

4 tbsp sherry vinegar

5 tbsp rice wine or sherry

1 tbsp clear honey

1 tsp chilli powder

125 ml/4 fl oz orange juice

4 tbsp lime juice

salt and pepper

freshly cooked noodles, to serve

lime wedges, to garnish

Season the chicken breasts on both sides with salt and pepper to taste, then roll them in the flour until coated. Heat the oil in a large frying pan. Add the garlic and cook, stirring, over a medium heat for 1 minute. Add the chicken, bay leaf, ginger and lemon grass and cook for 2 minutes on each side.

Add the vinegar, rice wine and honey, bring to the boil, then lower the heat and simmer, stirring occasionally, for 10 minutes. Add the chilli powder, then stir in the orange juice and lime juice. Simmer for a further 10 minutes. Using a slotted spoon, lift out the chicken and reserve. Strain and reserve the liquid and discard the bay leaf, then return the liquid to the pan with the chicken. Simmer for a further 15–20 minutes.

Remove from the heat and transfer to individual serving plates. Serve with freshly cooked noodles and garnish with lime wedges.

Chicken Chow Mein

serves 4

250 g/9 oz medium egg noodles

2 tbsp sunflower oil

275 g/9½ oz cooked chicken breasts, shredded

1 garlic clove, finely chopped

1 red pepper, deseeded and thinly sliced

100 g/3½ oz shiitake mushrooms, sliced

6 spring onions, sliced

100 g/3½ oz beansprouts

3 tbsp soy sauce

1 tbsp sesame oil

Place the egg noodles in a large bowl or dish and break them up slightly. Pour enough boiling water over the noodles to cover and leave to stand whilst preparing the other ingredients.

Heat the sunflower oil in a large preheated wok. Add the chicken, garlic, red pepper, mushrooms, spring onions and beansprouts to the wok and stir-fry for about 5 minutes.

Drain the noodles thoroughly. Add the noodles to the wok, toss well and stir-fry for a further 5 minutes.

Drizzle the soy sauce and sesame oil over the chow mein and toss until well combined.

Transfer to warmed serving bowls and serve immediately.

Cajun Chicken Gumbo

serves 2

1 tbsp sunflower oil

4 chicken thighs

1 small onion, diced

2 celery sticks, diced

1 small green pepper, deseeded and diced

85 g/3 oz long-grain rice

300 ml/10 fl oz chicken stock

1 fresh red chilli, thinly sliced

250 g/9 oz okra

1 tbsp tomato purée

salt and pepper

Heat the oil in a heavy-based frying pan and cook the chicken until golden. Remove the chicken from the pan using a slotted spoon. Stir in the onion, celery and green pepper and cook for 1 minute. Pour off any excess fat.

Add the rice and cook, stirring briskly, for a further minute. Add the chicken stock and bring to the boil.

Add the chilli and okra to the pan with the tomato purée. Season to taste with salt and pepper.

Return the chicken to the pan and stir. Cover tightly and simmer gently for 15 minutes, or until the rice is tender, the chicken is thoroughly cooked and all the liquid has been absorbed. Stir occasionally and if the mixture becomes too dry, add a little extra stock to moisten. Serve immediately.

Chicken & Spinach Lasagne

serves 4

350 g/12 oz frozen chopped spinach, thawed and drained

½ tsp ground nutmeg

450 g/1 lb lean cooked chicken, diced

4 sheets no-precook lasagne verde

1½ tbsp cornflour

425 ml/15 fl oz milk

4 tbsp freshly grated Parmesan cheese

salt and pepper

for the tomato sauce

400 g/14 oz canned chopped tomatoes

1 medium onion, finely chopped

1 garlic clove, crushed

150 ml/5 fl oz white wine

3 tbsp tomato purée

1 tsp dried oregano

salt and pepper

Preheat the oven to 200°C/400°F/Gas Mark 6.

To make the tomato sauce, place the tomatoes in a pan and stir in the onion, garlic, wine, tomato purée and oregano. Bring to the boil and simmer for 20 minutes until thick. Season to taste with salt and pepper.

Drain the spinach again and pat dry on kitchen paper. Arrange the spinach in the base of an ovenproof dish. Sprinkle with nutmeg and season to taste with salt and pepper.

Arrange the diced chicken over the spinach and spoon the tomato sauce over it. Arrange the sheets of lasagne over the tomato sauce.

Blend the cornflour with a little of the milk to make a paste. Pour the remaining milk into a pan and stir in the cornflour paste. Heat gently for 2–3 minutes, stirring constantly, until the sauce thickens. Season to taste with salt and pepper.

Spoon the sauce over the lasagne to cover it completely and transfer the dish to a baking sheet. Sprinkle the grated cheese over the sauce and bake in the preheated oven for 25 minutes until golden brown and bubbling. Serve immediately.

Mediterranean Chicken Parcels

serves 6

1 tbsp olive oil

6 skinless, boneless chicken breasts

250 g/9 oz mozzarella cheese, sliced

500 g/1 lb 2 oz courgettes, sliced

6 large tomatoes, sliced

1 small bunch of fresh basil leaves, torn

pepper

Preheat the oven to 200°C/400°F/Gas Mark 6. Cut 6 pieces of foil, each about 25 cm/10 inches square. Brush the foil squares lightly with oil and set aside until required.

With a sharp knife, slash each chicken breast at intervals, then place the mozzarella between the cuts in the chicken.

Divide the courgettes and tomatoes between the pieces of foil and season to taste with pepper. Scatter the basil over the vegetables in each parcel.

Place the chicken on top of each pile of vegetables, then wrap in the foil to enclose the chicken and vegetables, tucking in the ends.

Place on a baking tray and bake in the preheated oven for about 30 minutes.

To serve, unwrap each foil parcel and transfer the contents to warmed serving plates.

4

Entertaining

Roast Chicken

serves 6

1 chicken, weighing
2.25 kg/5 lb

55 g/2 oz butter

2 tbsp chopped fresh lemon
thyme

1 lemon, quartered

125 ml/4 fl oz white wine

salt and pepper

6 sprigs of fresh thyme,
to garnish

Preheat the oven to 220°C/425°F/Gas Mark 7. Make sure the chicken is clean, wiping it inside and out using kitchen paper, and place in a roasting tin.

Place the butter in a bowl and soften with a fork, then mix in the chopped thyme and season well with salt and pepper. Butter the chicken all over with the herb butter, inside and out, and place the lemon quarters inside the body cavity. Pour the wine over the chicken.

Roast the chicken in the centre of the oven for 15 minutes. Reduce the temperature to 190°C/375°F/Gas Mark 5 and continue to roast for a further 1¾ hours, basting frequently. Cover with foil if the skin begins to brown too much. If the tin dries out, add a little more wine or water.

Test that the chicken is cooked by piercing the thickest part of the leg with a sharp knife or skewer and making sure the juices run clear. Remove from the oven.

Remove the chicken from the roasting tin and place on a warmed serving plate to rest, covered with foil, for 10 minutes before carving.

Place the roasting tin on the top of the hob and simmer the pan juices gently over a low heat until they have reduced and are thick and glossy. Season to taste with salt and pepper.

Serve the chicken with the pan juices and scatter with the sprigs of thyme.

Coq au Vin

serves 4

55 g/2 oz butter

2 tbsp olive oil

1.8 kg/4 lb chicken pieces

115 g/4 oz rindless smoked
bacon, cut into strips

115 g/4 oz baby onions

115 g/4 oz chestnut
mushrooms, halved

2 garlic cloves, finely
chopped

2 tbsp brandy

225 ml/8 fl oz red wine

300 ml/10 fl oz chicken
stock

1 bouquet garni

2 tbsp plain flour

salt and pepper

bay leaves, to garnish

Melt half the butter with the oil in a large, flameproof
casserole. Add the chicken and cook over a medium heat,
stirring, for 8–10 minutes, or until golden brown all over.
Add the bacon, onions, mushrooms and garlic.

Pour in the brandy and set it alight with a match or taper.
When the flames have died down, add the wine, stock and
bouquet garni and season to taste with salt and pepper.
Bring to the boil, reduce the heat and simmer gently for
1 hour, or until the chicken pieces are cooked through and
tender. Meanwhile, make a beurre manié by mashing the
remaining butter with the flour in a small bowl.

Remove and discard the bouquet garni. Transfer the chicken
to a large plate and keep warm. Stir the beurre manié into
the casserole, a little at a time. Bring to the boil, return the
chicken to the casserole and serve immediately, garnished
with bay leaves.

Chicken Cacciatora

serves 4

1 chicken, about 1.5 kg/
3 lb 5 oz, cut into 6 or 8
serving pieces

125 g/4½ oz plain flour,
seasoned

3 tbsp olive oil

150 ml/5 fl oz dry white
wine

1 green pepper, deseeded
and sliced

1 red pepper, deseeded and
sliced

1 carrot, finely chopped

1 celery stick, finely
chopped

1 garlic clove, crushed

200 g/7 oz canned chopped
tomatoes

salt and pepper

Rinse and pat dry the chicken pieces with kitchen paper. Lightly dust them with the flour.

Heat the oil in a large frying pan. Add the chicken and cook over a medium heat until browned all over. Remove from the pan and set aside.

Drain off all but 2 tablespoons of the fat in the pan. Add the wine and stir for a few minutes. Then add the peppers, carrot, celery and garlic, season to taste with salt and pepper and simmer together for about 15 minutes.

Add the tomatoes to the pan. Cover and simmer for 30 minutes, stirring frequently, until the chicken is completely cooked through.

Check the seasoning before serving piping hot.

Chicken with Forty Cloves of Garlic

serves 6

1 chicken, weighing 1.6 kg/
3 lb 8 oz

3 garlic bulbs, separated
into cloves but unpeeled

6 sprigs of fresh thyme

2 sprigs of fresh tarragon

2 bay leaves

300 ml/10 fl oz dry white
wine

salt and pepper

cooked green beans,
to serve

Preheat the oven to 180°C/350°F/Gas Mark 4. Season the chicken inside and out with salt and pepper, then truss with fine string or elastic string. Place on a rack in a casserole dish and arrange the garlic and herbs around it.

Pour the wine over the chicken and cover with a tight-fitting lid. Cook in the preheated oven for 1½–1¾ hours, or until tender and the juices run clear when a skewer is inserted into the thickest part of the meat.

Transfer the chicken and garlic to a dish and keep warm. Strain the cooking juices into a jug. Carve the meat. Skim off any fat on the surface of the cooking juices.

To serve, divide the green beans between the serving plates and top with the chicken and garlic. Spoon over a little of the cooking juices and serve immediately.

Chicken Kiev

serves 4

115 g/4 oz butter, softened

3–4 garlic cloves, very finely chopped

1 tbsp chopped fresh parsley

1 tbsp snipped fresh chives

finely grated rind and juice of ½ lemon

8 skinless, boneless chicken breasts, about 115 g/4 oz each

55 g/2 oz plain flour

2 eggs, lightly beaten

175 g/6 oz dry breadcrumbs

groundnut or sunflower oil, for deep-frying

salt and pepper

Beat the butter in a bowl with the garlic, herbs, lemon rind and juice. Season to taste with salt and pepper. Divide into 8 pieces, then shape into cylinders. Wrap in foil and chill for about 2 hours, until firm.

Place the chicken between 2 sheets of clingfilm. Pound gently with a rolling pin to flatten the chicken to an even thickness. Place a butter cylinder on each chicken piece and roll up. Secure with cocktail sticks.

Place the flour, eggs and breadcrumbs in separate shallow dishes. Dip the rolls into the flour, then the egg and, finally, the breadcrumbs. Place on a plate, cover and chill for 1 hour.

Heat the oil in a saucepan or deep-fat fryer to 180–190°C/ 350–375°F, or until a cube of bread browns in 30 seconds. Deep-fry the chicken in batches for 8–10 minutes, or until cooked through and golden brown. Drain on kitchen paper. Serve immediately.

Green Chicken Curry

serves 4

2 tbsp groundnut or vegetable oil

4 spring onions, coarsely chopped

2 tbsp Thai green curry paste

700 ml/1¼ pints coconut milk

1 chicken stock cube

6 skinless, boneless chicken breasts, about 115 g/4 oz each, cut into 2.5-cm/1-inch cubes

large handful of fresh coriander, chopped

1 tsp salt

freshly cooked rice, to serve

Heat the oil in a preheated wok, add the spring onions and stir-fry over a medium-high heat for 30 seconds, or until starting to soften.

Add the curry paste, coconut milk and stock cube and bring gently to the boil, stirring occasionally. Add the chicken, half the coriander and the salt and stir well. Reduce the heat and simmer gently for 8–10 minutes until the chicken is cooked through and tender. Stir in the remaining coriander. Serve immediately with freshly cooked rice.

Chicken Tagine

serves 4

1 tbsp olive oil

1 onion, cut into small wedges

2–4 garlic cloves, sliced

450 g/1 lb skinless, boneless chicken breast, diced

1 tsp ground cumin

2 cinnamon sticks, lightly bruised

1 tbsp plain wholemeal flour

225 g/8 oz aubergine, diced

1 red pepper, deseeded and chopped

85 g/3 oz button mushrooms, sliced

1 tbsp tomato purée

600 ml/1 pint chicken stock

280 g/10 oz canned chickpeas, drained and rinsed

55 g/2 oz no-soak dried apricots, chopped

salt and pepper

1 tbsp chopped fresh coriander, to garnish

Heat the oil in a large saucepan over a medium heat. Add the onion and garlic and cook for 3 minutes, stirring frequently. Add the chicken and cook, stirring constantly, for a further 4 minutes, or until sealed on all sides. Add the cumin and cinnamon sticks and cook for a further minute.

Sprinkle in the flour and cook, stirring constantly, for 2 minutes.

Add the aubergine, red pepper and mushrooms and cook for a further 2 minutes, stirring constantly.

Blend the tomato purée with the stock, stir into the saucepan and bring to the boil. Reduce the heat and add the chickpeas and apricots. Cover and simmer for 15–20 minutes, or until the chicken is tender.

Season to taste with salt and pepper and serve immediately garnished with coriander.

Chicken Risotto

serves 4

4 tbsp butter

1 onion, chopped

125 g/4½ oz skinless, boneless chicken breasts, chopped

350 g/12 oz risotto rice

1 tsp ground turmeric

300 ml/10 fl oz white wine

1.2 litre/2 pints hot chicken stock

75 g/2¾ oz chestnut mushrooms, sliced

50 g/1¾ oz cashew nuts, halved

salt and pepper

Parmesan cheese shavings and fresh basil leaves, to garnish

Melt the butter in a large saucepan over a medium heat. Add the onion and cook, stirring, for 1 minute. Add the chicken and cook, stirring, for a further 5 minutes.

Add the rice and cook, stirring, for 15 minutes. Then add the turmeric, season to taste with salt and pepper, and mix well. Gradually stir in the wine, then stir in the hot stock, a ladleful at a time, waiting for each ladleful to be absorbed before stirring in the next. Simmer for 20 minutes, stirring from time to time, until the rice is tender and nearly all of the liquid has been absorbed. If necessary, add a little more stock to prevent the risotto drying out. Stir in the mushrooms and cashew nuts, and cook for a further 3 minutes.

Remove the risotto from the heat and spoon it into warmed serving dishes. Scatter over the Parmesan shavings and basil leaves and serve immediately.

Chicken with Linguine & Artichokes

serves 4

4 skinless, boneless chicken breasts

finely grated rind and juice of 1 lemon

2 tbsp olive oil

2 garlic cloves, crushed

400 g/14 oz canned artichoke hearts, drained and sliced

250 g/9 oz baby plum tomatoes

300 g/10½ oz dried linguine

chopped fresh parsley and freshly grated Parmesan cheese, to serve

Put each chicken breast in turn between 2 pieces of clingfilm and pound gently with a rolling pin to flatten to an even thickness. Put the chicken into a shallow dish with the lemon rind and juice and 1 tablespoon of the oil and turn to coat in the marinade. Cover and leave to marinate in the refrigerator for 30 minutes.

Put a large saucepan of water on to boil. Heat the remaining oil in a frying pan over a low heat, add the garlic and cook for 1 minute, stirring frequently. Add the artichokes and tomatoes and cook for 5 minutes, stirring occasionally. Add about half the marinade from the chicken and cook over a medium heat for a further 5 minutes. Cook the linguine in the boiling water for 8–10 minutes, or until tender but still firm to the bite.

Meanwhile, preheat the grill to high. Remove the chicken from the remaining marinade and arrange on the grill pan. Cook the chicken under the preheated grill for 5 minutes each side, until thoroughly cooked.

Drain the pasta and return to the saucepan, pour over the artichoke and tomato mixture and slice in the cooked chicken.

Divide between 4 warmed serving dishes and scatter over the parsley and Parmesan cheese.

Buttered Chicken Parcels

serves 4

4 tbsp butter

4 shallots, finely chopped

300 g/10½ oz frozen spinach, defrosted

450 g/1 lb blue cheese, such as Stilton, crumbled

1 egg, lightly beaten

1 tbsp snipped fresh chives

1 tbsp chopped fresh oregano

4 skinless, boneless chicken breasts

8 slices Parma ham

salt and pepper

baby spinach leaves, to serve

fresh chives, to garnish

Melt half of the butter in a frying pan over a medium heat. Add the shallots and cook, stirring, for 4 minutes. Remove from the heat and leave to cool for 10 minutes.

Preheat the oven to 180°C/350°F/Gas Mark 4. Using your hands, squeeze out as much moisture from the defrosted spinach as possible. Transfer the spinach into a large bowl, add the shallots, cheese, egg, herbs and salt and pepper to taste. Mix together well.

Halve each chicken breast then put each piece between 2 sheets of clingfilm and pound gently with a rolling pin to flatten to an even thickness. Spoon some cheese mixture into the centre of each piece, then roll it up. Wrap each roll in a slice of Parma ham and secure with a cocktail stick. Transfer to a roasting dish, dot with the remaining butter and bake in the preheated oven for 30 minutes until golden.

Divide the baby spinach leaves between 4 serving plates. Remove the chicken from the oven and place 2 chicken rolls on each plate. Garnish with fresh chives and serve.

Chicken Pinwheels with Blue Cheese & Herbs

serves 4

2 tbsp pine kernels, lightly toasted

2 tbsp chopped fresh parsley

2 tbsp chopped fresh thyme

1 garlic clove, chopped

1 tbsp grated lemon rind

4 skinless, boneless chicken breasts

250 g/9 oz blue cheese, such as Stilton, crumbled

salt and pepper

mixed salad leaves, to serve

lemon slices and sprigs of fresh parsley, to garnish

Put the pine kernels into a food processor with the chopped parsley, thyme, garlic and lemon rind. Season to taste with salt and pepper.

Put each chicken breast between 2 sheets of clingfilm and pound gently with a rolling pin to flatten to an even thickness. Spread them on one side with the pine kernel mixture, then top with the cheese. Roll them up from one short end to the other, so that the filling is enclosed. Wrap the rolls individually in aluminium foil, and seal well. Transfer to a steamer, cover tightly and steam for 10–12 minutes, or until cooked through.

Arrange the salad leaves on a large serving platter. Remove the chicken from the heat, discard the foil and cut the chicken rolls into slices. Arrange the slices on top of the salad leaves, garnish with lemon slices and sprigs of parsley, and serve.

Chicken & Veal Roll

serves 4

115 g/4 oz minced veal

4 skinless, boneless chicken breasts, about 125 g/4½ oz each

225 g/8 oz soft cheese flavoured with garlic and herbs

3 tbsp clear honey

salt and pepper

sage leaves, to garnish

Put the minced veal in a saucepan and cook over a medium-low heat, stirring frequently, for 5 minutes until evenly browned and broken up. Season to taste with salt and pepper and remove the pan from the heat. Leave to cool.

Preheat the oven to 190°C/375°F/Gas Mark 5. Spread out a sheet of clingfilm and place the chicken breasts on top, side by side. Cover with another sheet of clingfilm and beat gently with a meat mallet or rolling pin until the chicken forms a continuous sheet about 1 cm/½ inch thick.

Remove the chicken from the clingfilm and spread the cheese over one side of it. Spoon the minced veal evenly over the top. Roll up the chicken from one short side and brush with the honey.

Place the chicken roll in a roasting tin and cook in a preheated oven for 1 hour, or until tender and cooked through. Transfer the chicken roll to a chopping board and cut into thin slices.

Serve immediately, garnished with sage leaves.

Chicken in Marsala Sauce

serves 4

2 tbsp plain flour

4 skinless, boneless chicken breasts, sliced lengthways

3 tbsp olive oil

150 ml/5 fl oz Marsala

2 bay leaves

1 tbsp butter

salt and pepper

freshly cooked rice, to serve

Mix the flour with a little salt and pepper on a large plate or in a polythene food bag. Add the chicken and toss to coat.

Heat the oil in a frying pan over a medium heat. Add the chicken and cook for about 4 minutes on both sides until tender. Remove from the pan and keep warm.

Skim most of the fat from the pan and pour in the Marsala. Add the bay leaves and boil for 1 minute, stirring well, then add the butter with any juices from the chicken and cook until thickened.

Return the chicken to the pan and heat through. Serve immediately with freshly cooked rice.

Pan-fried Chicken with Golden Sauce

serves 4

2 mangoes

400 g/14 oz canned apricots in juice

55 g/2 oz unsalted butter

4 skinless, boneless chicken breasts, about 175 g/6 oz each

pepper

cooked new potatoes sprinkled with snipped chives, to serve

Using a sharp knife, slice off the sides of the mangoes as close to the stones as possible. Cut through the flesh in the half shells in a criss-cross pattern, turn inside out and cut off the flesh. Cut off any remaining flesh from the stones. Place in a food processor.

Drain the apricots, reserving 250 ml/9 fl oz of the can juice. Put the apricots and reserved juice into the food processor with the mangoes and process until smooth. Pour the sauce into a small saucepan.

Melt the butter in a large, heavy-based frying pan. Add the chicken and cook over a medium-low heat, turning occasionally, for 15 minutes until golden all over and cooked through. The juices should run clear when a skewer is inserted into the thickest part of the meat.

Meanwhile, place the saucepan of sauce over a low heat to warm through, but not boil.

Slice the chicken portions diagonally and arrange on warmed serving plates. Spoon the sauce over them and serve immediately with cooked new potatoes sprinkled with snipped chives and pepper to taste.

Roasted Chicken with Sun-blush Tomato Pesto

serves 4

4 skinless, boneless chicken breasts, about 800 g/1 lb 12 oz in total

1 tbsp olive oil

mixed salad, to serve

for the red pesto

125 g/4½ oz sun-blush tomatoes in oil (drained weight), chopped

2 garlic cloves, crushed

6 tbsp pine kernels, lightly toasted

150 ml/5 fl oz extra virgin olive oil

Preheat the oven to 200°C/400°F/Gas Mark 6. To make the red pesto, put the sun-blush tomatoes, garlic, 4 tablespoons of the pine kernels and the extra virgin olive oil into a food processor and blend to a coarse paste.

Arrange the chicken in a large, ovenproof dish or roasting tin. Brush the chicken breasts with the olive oil, then place a tablespoon of the red pesto on top of each. Using the back of a spoon, spread the pesto so that it covers the top of the chicken. (Store any remaining pesto in an airtight container in the refrigerator for up to 1 week.)

Roast the chicken in the preheated oven for 30 minutes, or until tender and the juices run clear when a skewer is inserted into the thickest part of the meat.

Sprinkle with the remaining pine kernels and serve with a mixed salad.

Tarragon Chicken

serves 4

4 skinless, boneless
chicken breasts, about
175 g/6 oz each

125 ml/4 fl oz dry white
wine

225–300 ml/8–10 fl oz
chicken stock

1 garlic clove, finely
chopped

1 tbsp dried tarragon

175 ml/6 fl oz double cream

1 tbsp chopped fresh
tarragon, plus extra
sprigs to garnish

salt and pepper

steamed mangetout,
to serve

Season the chicken with salt and pepper to taste and place in a single layer in a large, heavy-based frying pan. Pour in the wine and enough chicken stock just to cover and add the garlic and dried tarragon. Bring to the boil, reduce the heat and poach gently for 10 minutes, or until the chicken is cooked through and tender.

Remove the chicken with a slotted spoon or tongs, cover and keep warm. Strain the poaching liquid into a clean frying pan and skim off any fat from the surface. Bring to the boil and cook until reduced by about two-thirds.

Stir in the cream, return to the boil and cook until reduced by about half. Stir in the chopped fresh tarragon.

Slice the chicken breasts and arrange on warmed plates. Spoon over the sauce, garnish with sprigs of tarragon and serve immediately with steamed mangetout or other vegetables of your choice.

Chilli Chicken with Chickpea Mash

serves 4

4 skinless, boneless chicken breasts, about 140 g/5 oz each

1 tbsp olive oil

8 tsp harissa (chilli) paste

salt and pepper

for the chickpea mash

2 tbsp olive oil

2–3 garlic cloves, crushed

400 g/14 oz canned chickpeas, drained and rinsed

4 tbsp milk

3 tbsp chopped fresh coriander, plus extra to garnish

salt and pepper

Make shallow cuts in each chicken breast. Place the chicken in a dish, brush with the oil and coat both sides with the harissa paste. Season well with salt and pepper, cover the dish with foil and marinate in the refrigerator for 30 minutes.

Preheat the oven to 220°C/425°F/Gas Mark 7. Transfer the chicken breasts to a roasting tin and roast for about 20–30 minutes until they are cooked through and the juices run clear when a skewer is inserted into the thickest part of the meat.

Meanwhile, make the chickpea mash. Heat the oil in a saucepan and gently cook the garlic for 1 minute, then add the chickpeas and milk and heat through for a few minutes. Transfer to a blender or food processor and purée until smooth. Season to taste with salt and pepper and stir in the coriander.

To serve, slice the chicken breasts. Divide the chickpea mash between 4 serving plates, top each one with a sliced chicken breast and garnish with coriander.

Chicken with Saffron Mash

serves 4

550 g/1 lb 4 oz floury potatoes, cut into chunks

1 garlic clove, peeled

1 tsp saffron threads, crushed

1.2 litres/2 pints chicken or vegetable stock

4 skinless, boneless chicken breasts, trimmed of all visible fat

2 tbsp olive oil

1 tbsp lemon juice

1 tbsp chopped fresh thyme

1 tbsp chopped fresh coriander

1 tbsp coriander seeds, crushed

100 ml/3½ fl oz hot milk

salt and pepper

fresh thyme sprigs, to garnish

Place the potatoes, garlic and saffron in a large, heavy-based saucepan, add the stock and bring to the boil. Cover and simmer for 20 minutes, or until the potatoes are tender.

Meanwhile, brush the chicken breasts all over with half the oil and the lemon juice. Sprinkle with the chopped herbs and coriander seeds. Heat a griddle pan, add the chicken and cook over a medium-high heat for 5 minutes on each side, or until the juices run clear when a skewer is inserted into the thickest part of the meat. Alternatively, cook the chicken breasts under a preheated hot grill for 5 minutes on each side.

Drain the potatoes and return to the saucepan. Add the remaining oil and the milk, season to taste with salt and pepper and mash until smooth. Slice the chicken breasts diagonally. Divide the saffron mash between 4 large, warmed serving plates, top with the chicken and garnish with a few sprigs of fresh thyme. Serve immediately.